Contents

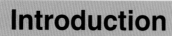

Introduction

The budgerigar is a small member of the parrot family which is extremely popular as a household pet, both kept individually and in pairs in cages, or in larger groups in an aviary. This guide is aimed at anyone that is interested in keeping a budgerigar as a pet, or already has some experience, but would like to learn more about them. We shall concentrate on keeping one or two birds indoors, rather than the more serious hobby of maintaining an aviary.

Understanding Budgerigars

Budgerigars are cheerful, cheeky little companions that enjoy relating to people. They are inexpensive to purchase and maintain, and are not generally prone to illness. They are suitable for owners of all ages, but the dust that they produce means that they should not be looked after by someone suffering from asthma, and should certainly not be kept in their bedroom.

Pet birds were often confined to their cages, generally on their own, for the whole of their lives. Nowadays, people are more enlightened, and most owners realise that pet birds should be allowed plenty of opportunity to fly outside of the confines of their cage, or be kept in a group in an aviary that provides enough space for them to fly around freely.

How Many?

In terms of pet budgies, the choice is between keeping them singly or in pairs. The only real advantage in keeping a budgie on its own is that it is much more likely to be able to learn to talk, especially if it is a male. If owning a talking bird is a priority, you will need to provide plenty of human companionship to replace that of other birds.

DID YOU KNOW?

The correct name for the keeping or rearing of birds is aviculture, after the Latin word avis for bird.

As budgerigars are naturally sociable in the wild, it seems that a pair of birds is ideal for a pet owner, and provided they grow up together, two birds of either sex will be good companions. A cock and a hen are also fine, and you may have the added delight of happy families of budgies, but you have to be prepared to find good homes for the regular clutches of offspring. Budgerigars can be mixed with other species of birds in an aviary, but care has to be taken to avoid bullying. They will usually mix well with canaries or other larger members of the finch family.

Budgies are naturally sociable and thrive if they are kept in pairs.

3

There are more than a hundred different colour varieties of budgie, all selectively bred from the original light-green type found in the wild. They are all pretty similar in hardiness and temperament, so the choice is very much one of personal preference.

Light Green

The basic budgerigar is similar to the wild type, but a bit larger. They have a light green body and yellow mask, shoulders and wings. The six throat spots, wing and head markings are black.

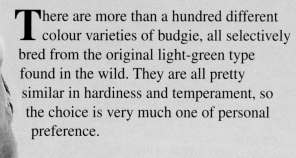

Light green, with a yellow mask, shoulders and wings.

Blue budgies come in a variety of shades.

DID YOU KNOW?

The oldest recorded pet budgerigar was Charlie, who lived to the grand old age of 29 years and 2 months in Stonebridge, London, born in 1948 and finally chirping his last on the 20th of June 1977. The normal life expectancy is from five to ten years.

The yellow buderigar.

Basic Colours

The four basic colours are Blue, White, Green and Yellow, but there are three shades of each of these colours, such as Sky Blue, Cobalt Blue and Mauve.

Crested Budgerigars

If you prefer a budgie that looks more ornate, then go for a crested. The fringe of feathers around their head make them look like they are wearing a badly fitting wig!

Albinos and Lutinos

Albino birds lack feather pigment and are totally white, whereas Lutinos are completely yellow. Both also lack pigment in the eyes, giving them a pink eye colour due to the blood vessels present in the iris.

Albino birds are totally white.

5

Buying a Budgerigar

The waxy cere around the nostrils is coloured brown in the female budgie (left), and coloured blue in the male.

DID YOU KNOW?

Perhaps the most famous talking budgie was Sparkie Williams, who had a repertoire of eight nursery rhymes, nearly 360 phrases, and a vocabulary of over 550 words. He died in 1962 – after becoming a star, selling over 20,000 copies of his record and featuring in many radio programmes.

A recognised breeder will often be very happy to sell on birds that are unsuitable for showing and breeding but will make perfect pets. Many pet stores sell budgerigars, but only use a shop that has a good reputation, is well kept, and where all the livestock look healthy and well-maintained.

Some shops specialise in the sale of pet birds, and the staff are likely to have a greater knowledge about birdkeeping than a more general store. (See the section on recognising signs of ill health in a budgerigar to assist with your choice.)

Show birds are often fitted with metal identification rings over their legs. These are of no real value to pet birds, but will do no harm provided they do not become too tight, in which case they can obstruct the blood supply to the foot and cause gangrene. If your bird has one, check it regularly to ensure it moves freely over the leg.

Male or Female?

Sexing a young bird is not easy. In adults, the waxy cere around the nostrils is blue in the case of the male, and brown in females. In youngsters it is a pink colour in the male, and bluish-white in the female.

What Age?

You should aim to buy a young bird of about six or seven weeks of age. Young birds have bars of colour running across the forehead, but these begin to disappear at about three months of age, when the cere also changes colour. Do not buy a bird after this age if you want to be able to train it.

Signs of a Healthy Budgie

Eyes: bright and clear

Feathers: sleek and well preened

Breathing: rapid, but quiet

Behaviour: chirpy and cheeky

Vent: a single opening common to the digestive, urinary and reproductive tracts, which should be clean

A healthy bird.

Breeders will usually keep their birds in a purpose-built aviary

DID YOU KNOW?

You could be reunited with a lost budgerigar if you teach it the address or the telephone number of your house. There have been cases of lost birds being reunited with their owners after reciting their details to the person who found them.

I would suggest that before you purchase a budgerigar you should pause to consider whether you want to own a pet that spends a life sentence behind bars, with only short opportunities to stretch its wings. Having a single bird confined to a relatively small cage is not fulfilling for either the budgerigar or its owner, but there are other options.

You could keep at least a pair of birds, and give them living quarters large enough for them to fly around easily. Alternatively, you should keep one or two birds in a cage, but allow them a great deal of freedom to fly around the room in which they live, when it is safe for them to do so.

Large cages are available for purchase as

'breeding cages', or can be manufactured from plywood with a wire-mesh front. They should be at least 3ft wide, 2ft high and 2ft deep (90 x 60 x 60cms). A wide range of wire-mesh cages can be purchased; the bars should be horizontal, rather than the vertical bars to be used for climbing. Avoid tall, narrow cages, as birds cannot fly vertically upwards!

Most wire cages have a removable sand tray in the bottom that can be slid in and out for cleaning. Plastic covers can be used to slip over the bottom of the cage to prevent excessive amounts of dust, droppings and seed husks from falling out.

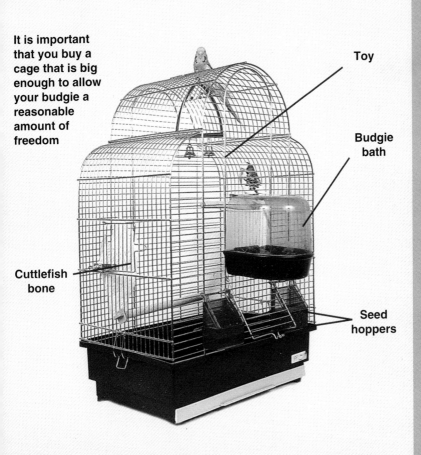

It is important that you buy a cage that is big enough to allow your budgie a reasonable amount of freedom

Toy

Budgie bath

Cuttlefish bone

Seed hoppers

Siting the Cage

Do not position the cage in direct sunlight, or in a draught. It should be covered at night to keep in the warmth and prevent the birds being startled if someone switches on the lights. Some house plants are poisonous to birds, and should be removed or covered when the birds are allowed out unattended.

On its first excursions, there is a danger that the bird may fly into a window and injure itself, so the curtains should be closed and any open fires should be guarded. The doors to the room can be protected with a bead or net curtain to prevent the bird flying out if it is accidentally left open. In many households, the birds can be left to fly free all day, just being shut into their cage again at night.

Fruit tree branches can make excellent perches.

Fixtures and Fittings

There are a wide range of budgie toys and accessories available for purchase, although some are designed as much for the owner as for the bird.

Disposable sandpaper makes cage cleaning an easy task.

FLOOR COVERING: The floor of the cage can be covered with sand, but most owners find it more convenient to use disposable sandpaper.

PERCHES: Budgerigars need perches close to each food and water pot. The standard half inch (12mm) dowling that is usually supplied is too narrow for many budgerigars. Lengths of fruit tree branch can make much better perches, and if they have varying thicknesses the birds can make their own choice.

LADDERS: Budgerigars love climbing, and as well as using the horizontal bars of the cage, they will use ladders to move from one level to another.

TOYS: Budgies do enjoy playthings, but it is better to supply a new one each day in rotation rather than cluttering the cage with a wide variety of toys. Something as simple as a table tennis ball can provide hours of fun. Plastic can sometimes splinter when pecked, so wooden toys are better.

Budgies that live on their own will sometimes spend many hours in front of a mirror, which is a sign that the bird is lonely rather than suffering from an over-inflated ego. They may even regurgitate food from their crop on to the mirror as a sign of their affection!

Your budgie will appreciate toys to play with.

Feeding Your Budgerigar

Seeds

Abudgerigar's natural diet is scrub grass which provides food when it seeds. Therefore, their basic diet in captivity should be mixed seeds. A wide variety of commercial products are available. Go for one that includes some seeds such as red rape, linseed or niger, as well as the more common canary seed and millet.

It is very important to blow away the husks that are left by the bird as it eats, or it may literally starve in the midst of plenty because it does not realise there is more seed underneath a layer of empty husks. The food dishes should be cleaned out daily, and the seed stored in a tightly-lidded container. Avoid buying very large packs of seed for just one or two birds, as the oil in the seed can easily go rancid.

Green Food

Fresh green foods are also appreciated, especially grass that is going to seed, chickweed, groundsel, dandelion and salad plants for human consumption. Ensure they have not been sprayed with any chemicals that may be harmful. Some birds also enjoy pecking at a slice of apple or carrot jammed between the bars of the cage.

Green food will be welcomed.

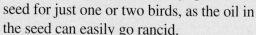

Millet

Sprays of millet are widely available, and are sometimes moulded with a binding agent such as honey into edible toys. They are fine in small quantities, but in excess can lead to obesity.

Grit

Birds have no teeth and do not chew the seed they eat after dehusking it. It passes down the gullet into a sac called the crop, then it enters the proventriculus, or stomach. It passes on to the gizzard, which is like a muscular grinding machine that contains grit to act as an abrasive. It is therefore essential that caged birds have access to some fine grit which they can eat to top up what they need to digest their food.

Budgies enjoy millet, but excess can lead to obesity.

Minerals

Budgerigars need quite a high mineral content in their diet, especially in the case of hens that are laying eggs. A cuttlefish bone, attached to the bars of the cage, will exercise the beak as well as supplying a valuable source of calcium. Iodine is also needed, and although most brands of budgerigar food do have iodine added, a mineral block containing iodine is useful.

A mineral block containing iodine (above) is a useful addition. Cuttlefish bones (right) are a good source of calcium.

Caring For Your Budgie

Cleaning the Cage

Budgerigars need to have their cage cleaned out regularly. The sand sheets need to be changed daily, empty seed husks and uneaten perishable food removed, and the water changed. If droppings have been deposited around the room after a free flight period, they will not stain the furniture if they are removed promptly. Once a week the cage needs a more thorough clean, with all furnishings and toys removed and washed, and the bars wiped with a damp cloth.

Preening

Budgerigars cannot preen themselves properly without being able to wet their feathers, and they naturally enjoy taking a dip. Special 'budgie baths' that attach to the cage can be purchased, but a saucer of water for splashing about is fine. Some budgies enjoy being sprayed with an atomiser of lukewarm water.

Budgies keep their feathers clean by preening. They need to wet their feathers in order to do this.

Beak and nails

If the perches are of a suitable diameter and the bird has access to a cuttlefish bone, the beak and nails should wear down naturally and never need clipping. Overgrown nails may interfere with the bird's ability to perch properly, and will be obvious if they are twisting out at abnormal angles.

You can clip the nails by holding them up to the light to see the pink quick that runs down the middle of the nail, and leaving about an eighth of an inch above that. If this is your first budgie, ask an experienced bird-keeper to help you. Ordinary nail-clippers can be used for the task. If a nail is cut too short, it may cause the bird some temporary discomfort and bleed for a while, but no lasting damage will result.

An overgrown beak can be more serious if it interferes with the bird's ability to pick up and de-husk its seed. Sometimes the upper and lower beaks grow completely out of alignment, and may then need clipping very often. It is best to ask a vet to do this, at least for the first time, so that you can see what is involved.

Training Your Budgie

L et your new budgie settle in for a day or two before you begin trying to handle it. A budgie learns best if it bonds with one particular member of the family, and providing it is purchased young enough, your budgie will learn to regard its owner as another member of its flock. Lots of regular attention from the outset will help to make the bird more tame. Make sure that the youngster is able to get to the feeding and water hoppers properly. Sprinkling some seed around the floor of the cage close by will help to attract them to the food supply, as will suspending a small spray of millet at the side of the feeding containers.

The correct way to hold a budgie.

Hand Training

The first step in training a budgerigar is to get it used to coming on to a finger. Get the bird accustomed to having your hand in the cage, and then put your outstretched index finger in front of its perch. It may well hop on to your finger, or you can gently push upwards on its body with your finger to encourage it.

You should get to the stage where the bird is happy to hop on to your finger before letting it out, so that you can return it to its cage with ease. Landing platforms can be purchased to fix on to the cage next to the door to make it easier for the bird to land and re-enter the cage on its own.

You should then progress to getting the budgie used to being held in one hand. First accustom the bird to being stroked along its back, then to having a hand gently laid upon it. You can then grasp the bird safely in the palm of your hand, with the first and second fingers controlling its head. Your other fingers and thumb should restrain the wings so they do not flap excessively. Any minor procedures such as nail and beak clipping, or the administration of medicines, can be carried out in this way.

Performing Tricks

Budgies can be taught to perform tricks, like 'Ring a bell' and 'Climb up a ladder', using actions of the finger that the bird will learn to mimic. Reward positive behaviour with a tasty treat. This type of training can be great fun, and helps to build up a bond between the bird and its owner.

It's Good to Talk...

A budgerigar will only be inclined to mimic human sounds if it is deprived of avian ones. Sexual equality means nothing to birds, and males are definitely better at small talk than females. Training a budgerigar to talk requires patience and persistence. Teaching the bird its name is a good place to start – but go for something easy, like 'Joey', rather than 'Aristotle'! The word must be repeated time and time again, and always with the same pronunciation and emphasis. Not all birds will learn to talk, and others will learn to mimic sounds around the house, such as the telephone ringing or even a dog barking.

Budgies can learn to talk, but a bird kept singly will probably be a better talker.

Breeding

DID YOU KNOW?

Budgerigars are native to Australia, where they rove over the dry interior plains in large flocks. The bird was introduced into Europe by the explorer and naturalist John Gould in 1840 and quickly became very popular. Nets were laid down on their feeding grounds to catch them, and large numbers died while being captured or during transport. All budgies now offered for sale have been bred in captivity.

DID YOU KNOW?

When they are first born, budgie chicks weigh just two grammes each.

When it comes to breeding, budgerigars are pretty laid back. Not for them the hard toil of building a fancy nest – in the wild they just lay their eggs in any convenient spot, such as a hollow in a tree, which will provide some protection and allow them to turn their eggs over regularly during the incubation period.

In captivity, each pair of birds should be provided with a nesting box with a base that contains a shallow depression to serve as a nest site. It should have a small round hole in the side for the hen to enter, with a perch situated just below it that the cock can use to feed her.

Budgerigars will pair off to breed, and the best time to allow them to mate is from about ten months of age. They can lay two or three clutches of around five eggs in a year. They are laid on alternate days, and they then hatch at intervals of two days after an eighteen-day incubation period.

The cock bird is usually very helpful during the incubation period, bringing food and regurgitating it for the hen to eat and then helping to feed the chicks by dehusking seeds for them. The youngsters develop very quickly, and by six weeks of age are fully fledged and ready to fly. They should not be handled before they are at least two weeks of age, but at that time it may be necessary to gently remove them to a cardboard box temporarily to clean out the nesting box.

A budgie will pine if it is left on its own.

Budgerigars need human company, particularly if they are kept singly. If a budgie in this situation is left alone, it will pine. Leaving a radio switched on will help for short periods. However, a budgie should not be left without supervision for more than a day or two. Food needs to be topped up regularly, empty husks must be cleared away, and the bird must be checked to ensure it is not showing any signs of being unwell.

Budgerigars have a very high metabolic rate, so they burn up a lot of energy for their size, and can quickly starve to death if they are not willing or able to eat regularly for any reason. A cage is easy to transport, so you can always take your budgie to a friend who could look after it while you are away. Leave clear written instructions of your bird's requirements and details of your vet, if relevant.

Budgies on the Move

You are likely to need to transport your budgerigar from time to time, at least to a veterinary surgery when it is unwell. Some people do take their budgies on holiday with them, which is fine in a caravan or self-catering accommodation, but they must not be left in excessively hot temperatures for any length of time, or they can suffer from heatstroke. A water-spray can help to keep the bird cool during a particularly hot journey.

Small travelling boxes can be purchased for transporting budgerigars. These are generally made out of cardboard with holes to allow air to circulate. These are fine for short journeys, but a standard-sized bird cage can also be used, covered with a light cloth to keep out draughts.

If you are going away, the best solution is to take your budgie to a friend who will look after it.

Health Care

Signs of Ill Health

● Behaviour – a sick budgie will be depressed and disinterested in its surroundings.
● Feathers – become ruffled and untidy if the bird is unwell.
● Vent – may become sore and caked with droppings.
● Eyes – may become dull or inflamed.
● Breathing – may become noisy and laboured, with a discharge from the nostrils.
● Skin – the skin over the legs and the cere (around the nose) may become crusty and sore.
● Feet – may become swollen, or the budgerigar may only perch on one leg.

Budgerigars can deteriorate very quickly when they are unwell, so regular inspection and prompt veterinary treatment are essential if the bird does appear

unwell. If you have more than one bird, isolate the sick one, and keep it in a cage somewhere really warm, such as an airing cupboard, until you can get it to a vet.

If the bird is not eating, you may be able to encourage it to take a little honey dissolved in water with a dropper, but do not force it to take the fluids against its will or it may inhale the fluid and develop pneumonia.

Administering Medication

Getting medication into a sick budgerigar is not easy. Some antibiotics come in the form of a soluble powder that can be added to the drinking water, but it can be difficult to ensure enough is taken. Medicated seed is an excellent way of administering drugs if the bird is eating, or drops can be given directly into the mouth. In some cases the only feasible route of administration is by injection.

DID YOU KNOW?

Birds are very susceptible to poisoning by fumes, which is why miners used to take canaries down the mines. They should be removed from the room if there is a lot of cigarette smoke or an open fire. Even the fumes from an over-heated non-stick saucepan can be highly toxic to a budgerigar.

Common Ailments

Scaly Face

Also known as scaly beak and scaly leg, because it causes crusting and scaling of these areas. It is caused by a little mite with the big name of Cnemidocoptes pilae, which is transmitted from bird to bird by direct contact and tunnels into the horny upper layer of skin. It is easily treated with a pesticidal preparation painted onto the affected areas, but severe deformities of the beak can result if it is not treated promptly.

Feather loss

There are many possible causes, including red mites, feather lice and other parasites, although these are not common in pet budgies. French moult is a condition that affects mainly young birds, where the feathers are deformed, often to the point where the bird is unable to fly. It is thought to be caused by a virus, and there is no known cure, although affected birds may be helped with a highly nutritious diet.

Perhaps the most common cause of feather loss in pet

budgerigars is feather plucking due to boredom, which can develop to the point where the bird plucks itself bald. Increasing the amount of stimulation and company that the bird receives may help, but in severe cases it may be necessary to fit the bird with a small plastic collar around its neck to restrain it until the habit is broken.

Growths

Unfortunately, these are very common in budgerigars, and can affect different parts of the body. Internal growths are a common cause of lameness, as they press upon the nerves to the leg. Tumours of the uropigial gland, which is situated under the tail and secretes the oils needed for preening, can cause swelling and bleeding under the tail. Fatty growths are also often seen on the abdomen, and can become very large before they interfere with the normal functioning of the bird.

Respiratory Infections

Psittacosis is the most serious disease that affects members of the parrot family as, although it often only causes mild respiratory signs in budgerigars, it can

DID YOU KNOW?

The budgerigar is the most widely kept companion bird in the world.

produce a severe form of pneumonia if passed on to humans. Fortunately, it is only common in newly imported birds, and so its incidence in pet budgerigars is very low.

There are several other causes of respiratory infections in pet budgerigars, causing noisy and laboured breathing, often with a bubbly discharge from the nostrils. Prompt treatment with antibiotics by a veterinary surgeon is essential as the condition can often be fatal.

Bumble Foot

This is the name given to a bacterial infection of the foot, causing it to become inflamed, swollen and tender. This can be very painful for the bird. Perches of the wrong diameter can play a part in causing the problem, and obesity will obviously aggravate it by putting more weight on the feet. In this case, the patient will need to cut down on fattening foods such as millet. A prolonged course of antibiotic treatment is often needed.

Egg Binding

Female birds will often lay eggs even in the absence of a mate, although they will obviously be infertile. Removing the eggs will simply encourage her to lay more to

replace them, so leaving them for her to try and incubate may be best. Sometimes the egg becomes stuck inside the hen, which will cause her to strain to try and pass it out. It may be visible just inside the cloaca. Veterinary assistance is usually necessary to try and clear the egg, sometimes it is even necessary to remove it surgically.

Goitre

This is an enlargement of the thyroid glands in the neck of the bird due to a deficiency of iodine in the diet. Budgerigars have a high requirement for iodine, but the condition has become much less common now that most budgies are fed on reputable brands of packeted bird seed.

It can develop if they are fed cheaper loose seeds without any added mineral supplements.

The pressure on the throat from the greatly enlarged glands can initially cause a loss of voice, and then difficulty with breathing. The bird may even become emaciated because it is unable to swallow seed properly. It is easily treated by

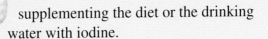

supplementing the diet or the drinking water with iodine.

Digestive Disorders

If your bird's droppings are very watery, an abnormal colour, or even tinged with blood, this could be due to enteritis, an inflammation of the bowel. A sudden change of diet may bring about the condition, and mild cases may settle down with a change back to plain seed.

More severe diarrhoea may be due to an infection, and sometimes a vet may need to carry out a laboratory examination of the droppings to establish the cause. Antibiotic seed is often given to clear any bacterial infections, and a medicine known as a probiotic can then be added to the drinking water to re-establish the normal, healthy bacteria in the gut.

Sour crop is a term given to an infection of the sac which is used to store the seed after it has been swallowed, and will cause the bird to keep regurgitating foul smelling food. A dilute solution (2 per cent) of

chlorhexidine antiseptic in the drinking water may clear the problem, but antibiotics from a vet are often needed.

Surgery for Budgies

Birds present particular difficulties to a veterinary surgeon trying to anaesthetise them, and there is no doubt that they are at a higher surgical risk than many other animals. Despite this, it is now not uncommon for surgical procedures, such as tumour removal, to be successfully carried out in budgerigars.

There are veterinary surgeons that have a special interest in the treatment of birds, and if your own vet is reluctant to carry out an operation despite there being some realistic hope of success, you could ask to be referred to a vet that has the specialised expertise and equipment needed. But beware – the cost of this type of treatment is likely to be many times the cost of buying a new bird!